Toadstools and Such

by SOLVEIG PAULSON RUSSELL

Illustrated by Joe Nerlinger

STECK-VAUGHN COMPANY • AUSTIN, TEXAS

ISBN 0-8114-7711-8
Library of Congress Catalog Card Number 73-110691
Copyright © 1970 by Steck-Vaughn Company, Austin, Texas
All rights reserved. Printed and bound in the United States of America

1609198

TABLE OF CONTENTS

INTRODUCTION

Toadstools and mushrooms are the same strange plants.

   Toadstools is a name that is often given to mushrooms. Mushrooms grow in many places. They can be found in woods, in parks, and on grassy lawns. They are found growing in damp places or swamps, on hills and the sides of mountains, and on and among certain trees. Some of the strange plants grow on decaying logs, and some are even found on sawdust heaps.

The plants may be black, orange, lavender, yellow, pink, rosy red, brown, green, blue, or white or flesh colored. Often the under parts are not the same color as the tops. Some plants have spots and streaks of different colors.

Mushroom tops, or caps, have interesting and different shapes.

half circle   bell

peaked hat   funnel   ball

fan   sponge   sea coral

The name *toadstool* comes from an ancient word referring to the plant's shape and legends associating it with toads.

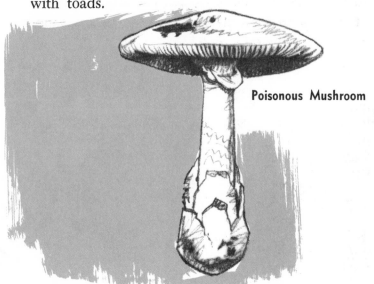

Poisonous Mushroom

It is very difficult to tell poisonous and nonpoisonous mushrooms apart.

Nonpoisonous Mushrooms

The name *mushroom* comes from a Latin word *mus-sirion* (mus-*ir*-i-on), and the eating of mushrooms dates back to the time of ancient Rome. The Emperor Nero is said to have served poisonous mushrooms at a banquet and murdered his guests.

One mushroom that was not poisonous was called the "mushroom of the Caesars," and it was served only on gold and silver plates.

Many mushrooms can be eaten, but it must be remembered that some, like the ones which Nero served, are deadly poisonous.

Mushrooms found in a grocery store are the safest ones to eat!

MUSHROO

CLASSIFICATION

Mushrooms are different from other plants.

Mushrooms are plants, but they are not green plants. They have no roots or leaves as green plants do, and they never have any flowers.

The mushrooms that are seen growing out of the ground are only the fruit parts of some of the large group of plants called FUNGI (*funj*-eye).

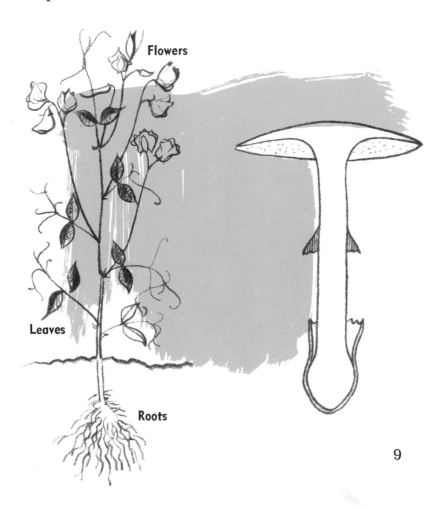

Flowers

Leaves

Roots

9

The word *fungus* comes
from a Greek word meaning
"sponge." Some of the plants
look like sponges.

Higher Plants

People who study about fungi are MYCOLOGISTS (my-
col-o-gists). They believe that some fungi were among
the first plants on earth, long before more complex green
plants developed. Fungi are classified as "lower plants"
because of their simple parts.

KINDS OF FUNGI

There are thousands of kinds of fungi.
Some are useful.

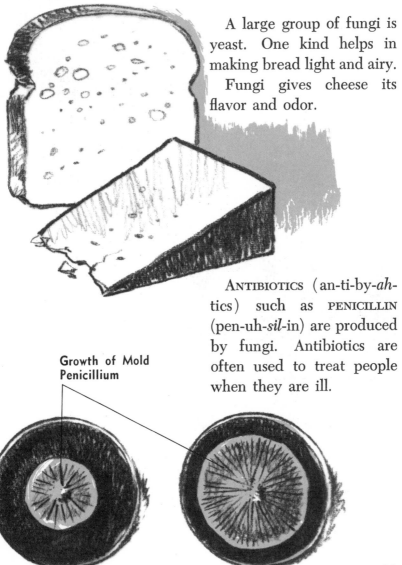

A large group of fungi is yeast. One kind helps in making bread light and airy. Fungi gives cheese its flavor and odor.

ANTIBIOTICS (an-ti-by-*ah*-tics) such as PENICILLIN (pen-uh-*sil*-in) are produced by fungi. Antibiotics are often used to treat people when they are ill.

Growth of Mold
Penicillium

Some fungi are harmful.

The molds that are some-times found growing on food are fungi.

Fungi called "smuts" and "rusts" may spoil a field of corn, wheat, or other grain.

Ringworm and athlete's foot are caused by fungi that may live on the human body.

SIZE OF FUNGI

Fungi grow in many different sizes.

Size of fungi varies. Some fungi, such as yeast cells, can only be seen with a microscope.

Small mushrooms may have caps as little as one-half inch wide. Other mushroom caps are from one to eight or more inches wide.

Some puffballs are the largest of the fungi.

COMPARISON OF GREEN PLANTS AND FUNGI

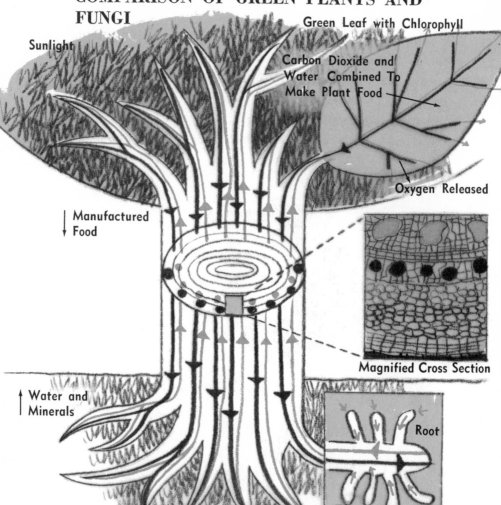

Sunlight

Green Leaf with Chlorophyll

Carbon Dioxide and Water Combined To Make Plant Food

Oxygen Released

Manufactured Food

Magnified Cross Section

Water and Minerals

Root

Unlike the fungi, most of the plants around us are green and grow in the sunshine. They draw their food from the soil and air and change it into growing greenness. They can do this because they have a substance called CHLOROPHYLL (*chlor*-uh-phil).

14

Fungi do not grow like green plants.

Fungi, not having the parts and chlorophyll that green plants have, must grow in a different way. Since they cannot make their own food, mushrooms and other fungi must live off other plants and animals. That is the reason many mushrooms are found in places where there are decaying leaves and plants they can feed upon.

Other fungi grow on living things, such as trees.

15

In fungi, spores take the place of seeds.

Most green plants grow seeds with which they reproduce their own kind. All the flowering plants—fruits, vegetables, trees, grains, and grasses—produce seeds.

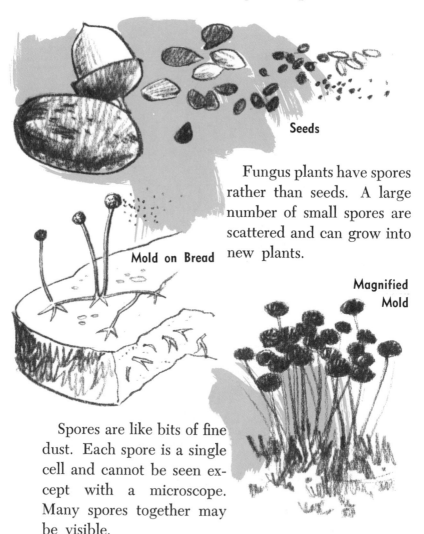

Seeds

Fungus plants have spores rather than seeds. A large number of small spores are scattered and can grow into new plants.

Mold on Bread

Magnified Mold

Spores are like bits of fine dust. Each spore is a single cell and cannot be seen except with a microscope. Many spores together may be visible.

16

HOW SPORES GROW INTO MUSHROOMS

Spores may be blown about by the wind for days.

What happens when a tiny spore of a common mushroom finally settles down in a moist place and begins to grow into a new plant?

The spore first divides into two cells, or parts. Then each of these cells divides again into two more parts each, and each new part keeps dividing and dividing. A tiny thread appears.

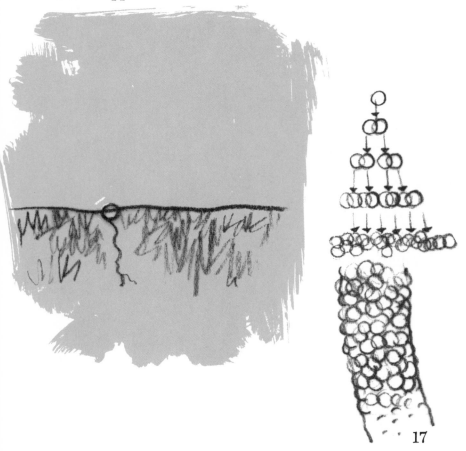

17

Part of the mushroom grows underground.

Soon long, thin chains are formed and become a mass of tangled, tubelike threads going in every direction. This mass of threads under the ground is called the MYCELIUM (my-*see*-li-um), from a Greek word for mushroom.

The mycelium takes the place of roots, stems, and leaves of a green plant. It actually is the whole plant, except for the part above the ground that makes the spores. The mycelium is the food-gathering part of the fungus, for it absorbs moisture and food from its surroundings through the walls of the cells.

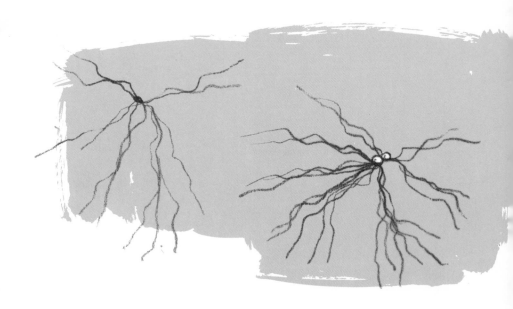

Part of the mushroom grows above ground.

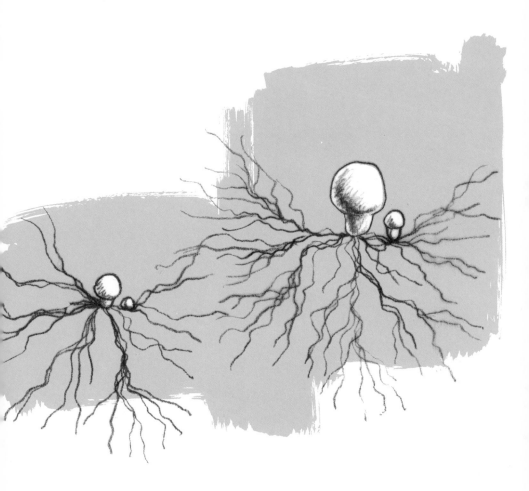

When the mycelium has developed far enough, some of the threads near the surface bunch together to form small knots. The knots grow, taking on rounded shapes and swelling. Soon they grow through the surface and become button mushrooms. The button then grows upward into a stem and a cap.

19

Sometimes the mass of underground threads keeps spreading to form a large circle, and mushrooms appear in a ring. These are called "fairy rings" and may become as large as a hundred feet across.

Although the fairy ring may appear overnight, the mycelium has been under the ground for many years, perhaps even centuries. Mushrooms grow out of the mycelium only when the right conditions of moisture and temperature are present.

According to European folk tales, the rings marked the places where fairies had danced. Stepping inside a ring of mushrooms was supposed to bring good luck.

Gills with
Spores

Many mushrooms have a small circular cap under which little sections grow outward like the spokes of a wheel. These thin, knife-like growths are gills, and they are covered with spores.

Some mushrooms have an underside made up of tiny rounded tubes that hold the spores until ripe.

Gilled mushrooms have parts that correspond to the parts of an umbrella.

21

HOW MUSHROOMS BEAR SPORES

Mushrooms bear their spores in different ways.

Most mushrooms bear spores on the surface of microscopic cells which look like small club-shaped holders. Gilled mushrooms, bracket mushrooms, and puffballs are club fungi.

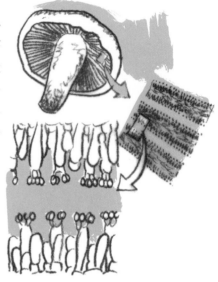

Magnified Spores

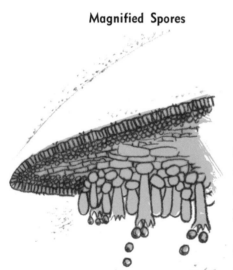

Members of the club fungi shed their spores in different ways. Most spores are dropped, but some are exploded into the air.

When puffballs are ripe, they burst open and shoot out their spores.

22

Magnified Spores

Other mushrooms bear their spores in microscopic sacs. Sponge mushrooms, or spring morels, are members of the sac fungi. The spores are shed from the sacs within the wrinkles and ridges of the cap.

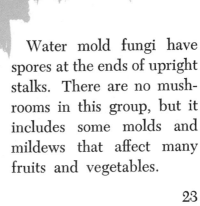

Water mold fungi have spores at the ends of upright stalks. There are no mushrooms in this group, but it includes some molds and mildews that affect many fruits and vegetables.

23

HOW MUSHROOM SPORES ARE TRANSPORTED

Spores may travel as far away as another continent.

When the dustlike spores are ripe, they fall from the mushroom and are blown away by any puff of wind.

Spores also may be carried away by animals or insects which may touch them.

24

Millions of spores come from each mushroom. Most of them will not land in a place where they can grow. But because there are so many spores, some will find just the right conditions for growing.

A mushroom dies and decays after shedding its spores.

MAKING A SPORE PRINT

If you can find a gilled mushroom growing, you can make a print of its spores. Look for one with colored spores because they can be seen more easily. Cut the cap off the mushroom and place it on a piece of plain paper. Do not use a slick, shiny paper as the spores will not stick to it. Be sure that the gill part of the cap touches the paper.

Over the cap place a glass or jar and leave it overnight. When you lift the glass and cap, you will see that spores have dropped to the paper, making a spore print.

Spore prints look something like the spokes of a wheel. Examine your print with a magnifying glass.

Be sure to wash your hands after handling mushrooms.

VARIETIES OF MUSHROOMS

Puffballs

Puffballs are one of the mushrooms that do not have gills for their spores.

The young plants that grow from the mycelium just keep expanding like small balloons. The firm, white insides of the puffballs gradually turn dark as the plant grows and the spores ripen. When the spores are fully ripe, the outside of the ball cracks, and the dusty brown spores are forced out. Ripe puffballs were once called "Devil's Snuffboxes" and "Smokeballs."

Puffballs are not poisonous, and they may be eaten when the insides are white and firm.

28

Pasture puffballs are about the size of a baseball.

The little puffballs that look like spinning tops are about two inches wide and grow in little clusters.

Giant puffballs are rare. They can grow to be six feet around and weigh more than twenty pounds. In the days before matches were invented, the dried insides of these huge balls were often used as tinder to start fires.

Earthstars look like round puffballs at first, but later their outer skin splits into star-shaped points which fold back to show a little central ball which contains spores.

An unusual earthstar is the water-measurer. During wet weather, the points of the plant rest upon the ground. Dry weather causes the points to curl up over the center.

Natives in Central America once used the earthstar mushroom to treat infected wounds.

The stinkhorn mushrooms have an unpleasant smell. The tip is covered with a sticky substance which has the spores imbedded in it. Insects such as flies and beetles are attracted to the plant and eat the covering. They carry off the stink-horn's spores on their bodies.

Fly Amanita

Parasol-like mushrooms, such as the poisonous fly amanita (am-ah-*nih*-ta), may have stems twenty inches long. They can grow singly or in groups, but they never grow in clusters as some mushrooms do. There are many kinds of parasol-shaped mushrooms.

Honey Agaric

The golden-colored honey agaric (*ag*-uh-rik) looks like a flower. It may be found growing in small clusters on stumps and on the buried roots of trees.

The Blushing Amanita

Like the fly amanita, the blushing amanita is also poisonous. It received its name because it slowly changes from white to red when it is bruised or stepped on.

The Shaggy-Mane

Quite often found on lawns, the shaggy-mane has an unusual appearance. It is white and covered with yellowish scales. The plant gradually turns black. The shaggy-mane is not poisonous.

Bird's Nest Mushrooms

Some of the unusual-shaped mushrooms look like little cups or goblets or like a bird's nest filled with tiny eggs.

Coral Mushrooms

Some mushrooms resemble the coral that grows in ocean water.

Bracket Mushrooms

The bracket mushroom grows from trees and logs in the shapes of fans or little shelves. The caps are spreading and flat.

When you walk through the woods or parks, you may see bracket mushrooms growing on the trees.

Some look like blobs of dough or biscuits.

Some look like folded ears or saddles.

And one bracket mushroom looks like an oyster.

Pine Cone Mushroom

In July or August the pine cone mushroom may be found hidden in the woods.

Hedgehog Mushrooms

Often called the "tooth" mushroom, the hedgehog mushroom has unbranched "teeth" growing downward upon which the spores are located. The long teeth give the plant a lacy appearance.

TRUFFLES

The unusual fungi called truffles grow underground.

Truffles are not mushrooms, but they are interesting fungi. They grow underground at the base of certain kinds of trees. There are different varieties of truffles, and most are found from three to four inches under the ground. When they grow near the surface, they may crack the ground or push the earth upward in little mounds. Usually truffles weigh only a few ounces, but occasionally one weighs more than a pound.

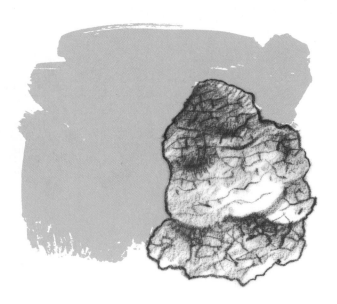

It is not easy to find the dark, irregularly shaped truffles that look like tiny brown balls with thick rough "hides" or skins. They are hidden treasure for those who find them since they are considered a fine food.

Animals like to eat truffles, too. Wild boars, deer, bears, goats, badgers, squirrels, and mice dig up the truffles for food. The animals can smell this unusual fungus even though it grows underground.

Even insects are attracted to the smell of the underground plants, and they are sometimes seen swarming above the ground where truffles are growing.

Pigs were once used to hunt truffles.

For hundreds of years people of Europe used pigs as truffle hunters. They took a pig to the forest, tied a rope on its neck, and then let the pig sniff and hunt until it smelled the hidden truffles.

When the pig began to root out the plant, the owner tied the pig, gave it some reward such as a few acorns, and dug up the truffles for himself.

Once the selling of truffles was important in France, England, and other countries; but with the growth of cities the woodlands became scarce. The old truffle business has gradually almost died out.

40

GROWING MUSHROOMS FOR FOOD

Mushrooms have been grown by men for food for about four hundred years. They were first grown in France in old caves where the moisture and temperature were even and where there was a constant, gentle movement of air. There were almost no mushrooms grown in the United States until about 1900, but at the present time this country leads the world in growing mushrooms.

There are tons of mushrooms grown and picked every day in the United States. They are raised in cool, dark buildings, in caves, and sometimes in old mines. They are canned or sold to be eaten fresh.

Growing mushrooms is not easy. Spores from mushrooms must be planted in beds of compost, a mixture of rich soil and decaying matter. Temperature and moisture must be kept just right, and the beds must be changed when the soil becomes worn out by mushroom growth.

The mushrooms must be picked by hand by people who can tell when the plants are at their best. Sometimes insects ruin the beds.

The plants are not allowed to grow to full size before being harvested. Usually only the partially grown plants, or buttons, are selected.

Mushrooms may be cooked with butter and served by themselves; or they may be combined with other foods in sauces, soups, and various dishes.

Large mushrooms are prepared in special ways and are considered a delicacy.

A MUSHROOM HUNT

It is fun to hunt and study these unusual plants.

TIME: After a heavy rain in spring, fall, or summer
PLACE: On lawns, parks, woods—wherever green plants
        are growing—and around tree trunks or on fallen
        or decayed wood

The first rule a mushroom hunter will remember is that *there is no sure way to tell a poisonous mushroom from one that can be eaten.* Mushrooms are collected only for fun and study. One bite into a very poisonous mushroom can be fatal.

Take cloth bags or sacks to carry the mushrooms and try to keep the different types separate. Hands should always be washed after handling the plants.

Collect only the fully grown mushrooms. Buttons of mushrooms that can be eaten and of poisonous ones often look exactly alike.

Carry this book to see if you can find any of the varieties of mushrooms pictured.

Signs that may point to poisonous mushrooms.

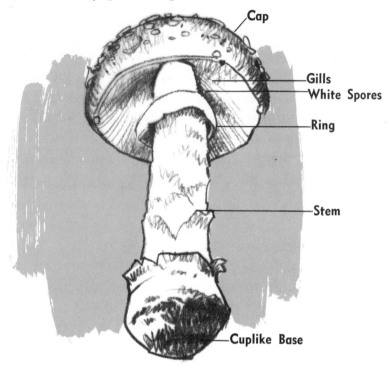

1. The base of the stem has a part that looks like a cup holding it. This cuplike base is near the ground or may be under it.
2. There is a ring around the stem of the mushroom just below the cap.
3. The gills are not touching the stem but are located in the cap.
4. The spores are white.

Remember that there are other poisonous mushrooms that may not have any of these characteristics, and there are mushrooms which can be eaten that may have some of them.

In a notebook write down the following information about each mushroom you find.

General Description and Shape: Tell if the mushroom is shaped like an umbrella, a ball, a bell, a funnel, a piece of coral, a star, a nest of bird's eggs, a honeycomb, a little fan, or whatever shape you think the mushroom most closely resembles.

Does it have a dull or waxy appearance? Is there a milky fluid in the plant? Does the plant glow in the dark?

Method of Growing: Does the plant grow by itself, in groups, or clustered in tufts on wood?

Place of Growth: Note if the mushroom was found on the ground, in the open, in the woods, by trees, on tree trunks, among fallen leaves, or elsewhere.

Time of Year: Write down the date, the season of the year, and the temperature.

Size: Measure the length of stems and the width of caps. An ordinary tape measure may be used.

Color: Note colors of stems, caps, gills, and spores.

Smell: Some mushrooms have an unpleasant smell. See if you detect an odor about each plant.

45

EXPERIMENTS WITH FUNGI

Type of Fungus: Water molds

Location:

In water and in the air

Example:

The gray fungus often seen on fish

Simple Experiment:

Drop a dead fly into an aquarium. Use pond water. What do you see growing on the fly after a few days?

Type of Fungus: Yeasts, mildews, molds

Location:

In the air, on green plants, and on citrus fruits

Examples:

Yeast cells in the air

Diseases of plants and fruit

Simple Experiment:

Leave a glass of fruit juice exposed to the air. What change do you notice after a day or so? Yeast cells brought about the change.

Observe diseased plants and fruits, such as peas, roses, oranges, and apples. What is the mildew or mold doing to the plant?

46

Type of Fungus: Mushrooms

Location:

On the ground, on trees, in the open or in the woods, and around tree stumps

Example:

Common field mushroom

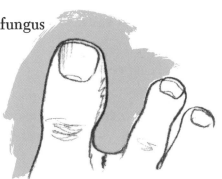

Simple Experiment:

Carefully transplant some of the mycelium obtained from the common field mushroom into a tray of compost obtained from your local nurseryman. Keep the tray in a basement or any dark, cool place where the temperature will be around 55 degrees. The tray must be watered just enough to keep the compost from becoming dry.

In a few days, what is the white growth you see?

Type of Fungus: Imperfect fungus

Location:

On living things, plants, animals, and human beings

Examples:

Ringworm and athlete's foot

Observation Only:

Observe this fungus as it lives on living things, but do not experiment. Why do you think ringworms are contagious?

THE ROLE OF FUNGI IN NATURE

Fungi dispose of decaying plant life.

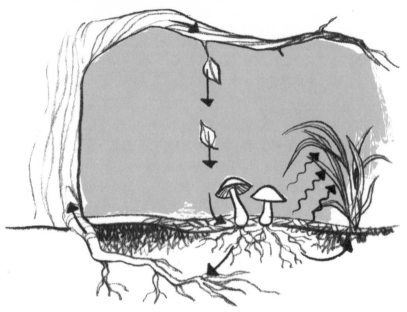

It is fun to look for the strange plants called mushrooms and to learn about them. One of the interesting things we learn is that without the world of fungi and bacteria (one-celled organisms) there would be no way of disposing of all the fallen leaves, branches, and old trees in the forest. A single growing tree would soon be covered with its own fallen leaves.

The fungi help decompose, or break down, the leaves—and all former living matter—thus enriching the soil and at the same time providing for their own food. The breaking down of old plant life releases a gas that is reused by living plants. There is no waste in nature, and the fungi have an important role in nature's plan.

48